The Modern Speller, Book 1 - Primary Source Edition

Kate Van Wagenen

Nabu Public Domain Reprints:

You are holding a reproduction of an original work published before 1923 that is in the public domain in the United States of America, and possibly other countries. You may freely copy and distribute this work as no entity (individual or corporate) has a copyright on the body of the work. This book may contain prior copyright references, and library stamps (as most of these works were scanned from library copies). These have been scanned and retained as part of the historical artifact.

This book may have occasional imperfections such as missing or blurred pages, poor pictures, errant marks, etc. that were either part of the original artifact, or were introduced by the scanning process. We believe this work is culturally important, and despite the imperfections, have elected to bring it back into print as part of our continuing commitment to the preservation of printed works worldwide. We appreciate your understanding of the imperfections in the preservation process, and hope you enjoy this valuable book.

THE MODERN SPELLER

BOOK ONE

BY

KATE VAN WAGENEN, Pd.B.

PRINCIPAL PUBLIC SCHOOL No. 53, BOROUGH OF MANHATTAN
NEW YORK CITY

AUTHOR OF "DICTATION DAY BY DAY"

New York
THE MACMILLAN COMPANY
1916

All rights reserved

HARVARD COLLEGE LIBRARY
GIFT OF
GINN & COMPANY
MARCH 17, 1927

COPYRIGHT, 1916,
BY THE MACMILLAN COMPANY.

Set up and electrotyped. Published March, 1916.

Norwood Press
J. S. Cushing Co. — Berwick & Smith Co.
Norwood, Mass., U.S.A.

PREFACE

THE MODERN SPELLER emphasizes the following points:

Teaching Spelling by the Dictation Method. It is a well-known fact that children write a word correctly in a list, and write the same word incorrectly in a sentence. This difficulty exists because the sentence form is strange. When a pupil learns *this, see, ball*, as a list, the spelling of these three words constitutes the sum of the information gained in that lesson; but if he writes, *See this ball*, he has taken the first step in composition. It is because of this great gain that in all modern schools, teachers are beginning to recognize the advantages of teaching spelling by the dictation method.

Grading. The exercises are carefully graded so that the vocabulary, the context, and the punctuation marks are suited to the needs and abilities of the pupils. In addition, each new lesson contains but a few new words, which are placed in the margin. Every other word in the lesson is a review word.

Reviews. The dictation method, requiring the constant repetition of small, troublesome words, linked with the close grading mentioned above, constitutes a natural review. In addition, reviews are inserted in the earlier years at the close of every fourth lesson.

Meaning and Use of Words Taught from Text. As the average person obtains his knowledge of the meaning and use of words from reading, children should be urged and encouraged to learn the meaning of words, as far as possible, by reference to the context.

Interesting Content. The subjects dwelt upon interest the pupil, and, if properly handled, pave the way for superior composition work. Some literary exercises are introduced, but they have not been permitted to overshadow the fact that the Modern Speller is designed primarily to teach spelling.

These lessons were used in manuscript form for several terms. The teachers put the exercises on the blackboard and the children copied them for home study. It was found, however, that this method wasted time — a fault that in our crowded curriculum seems almost a crime. A far weightier objection to this method was the fact that in classes, even of careful teachers, many children made mistakes in copying the exercises. They, therefore, studied them incorrectly; so that the teacher, besides dealing with legitimate difficulties, bore the added burden of eradicating errors that were firmly fixed in the pupil's mind. To overcome these two difficulties a book was prepared so that every child might have a printed page from which to study.

Thanks are due the following authors and publishers for permission to use copyrighted material: to Harper Brothers for the selections from Margaret Sangster's " Little Knights and Ladies "; to A. P. Watt & Son for the selection from Kipling's " Jungle Book "; to A. S. Barnes & Co. for the selection from the Teachers' Magazine; to the Public School Publishing Co. for the selection from McMurry's " Classic Stories."

The selections from " Sermons to Young Men " and " Stories of the Psalms " by Henry van Dyke, and " Poems and Ballads " by R. L. Stevenson, are used by permission of Charles Scribner's Sons, the authorized publishers of the works of these authors.

The selections from Holmes, Larcom, Longfellow, Lowell, and Cary are used by permission of Houghton Mifflin Company, the authorized publishers of the works of these authors.

SUGGESTIONS TO TEACHERS

The work of each year has been divided into two parts, and can be accomplished in the given time if the proper method is employed. One dictation exercise constitutes a day's lesson; but, in addition, assign three or four words from the review lists which follow every fourth lesson. When the four dictations and the review have been taught, review the week's work and teach no new matter. Keep a list of the words misspelled daily, and on Friday drill on these. Do not waste time by repeating again and again what all the children know.

The words in the margin are the only new words in any lesson. Occasionally a review word is even inserted here to show the formation of plurals or of participles.

The first year that spelling is taught, allow no home work, but arrange, instead, two spelling periods a day. Use the morning for oral spelling and for copying both words and sentences two or three times, and the afternoon for oral spelling and the dictation of the sentences. At the beginning of the Third Year, home work may be assigned; but only after a thorough explanation on the part of the teacher.

Whenever unusual proper names, as Gessler, Siegfried, etc., have not been placed in the margin, it is because they are not to be taught; but it is wise to put them on the blackboard and permit them to remain there during the writing of the lesson.

Funk & Wagnalls' Standard Dictionary is the authority used in this book for spelling and syllabication.

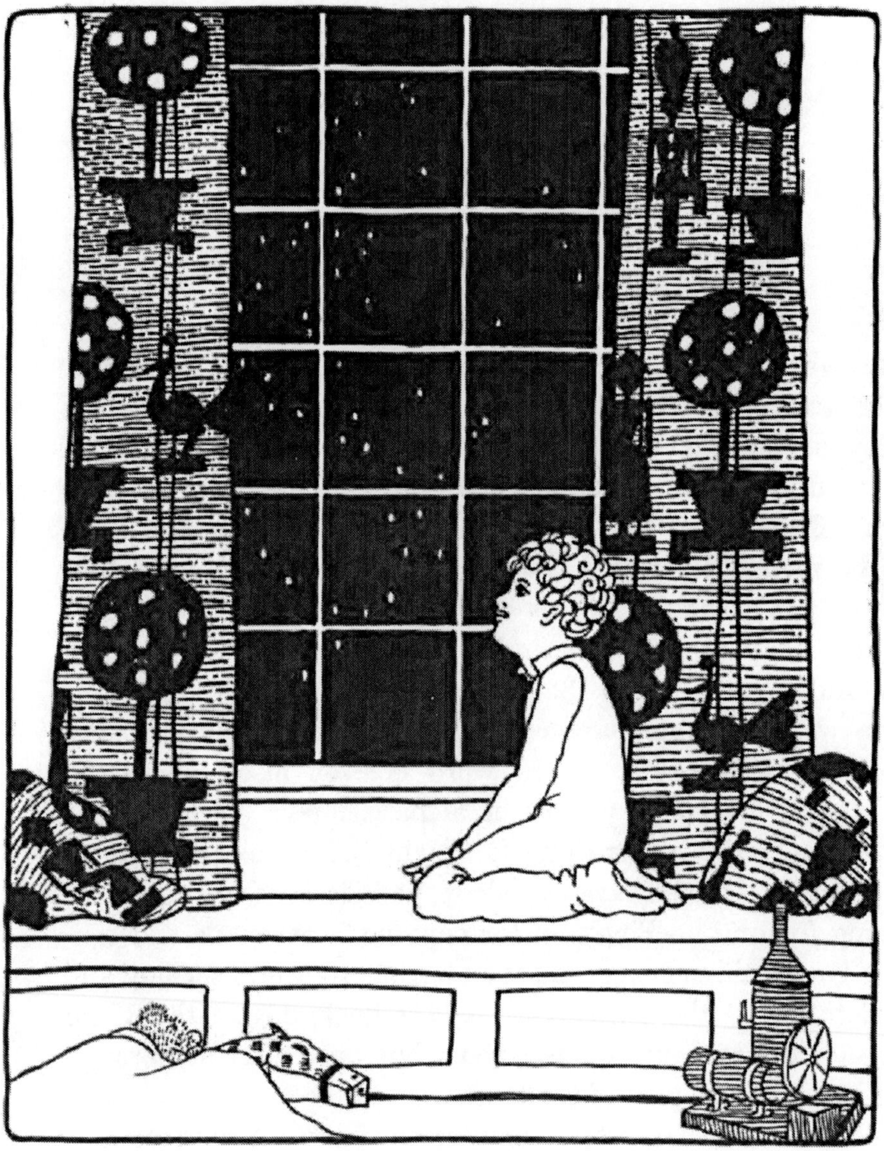

SECOND YEAR — FIRST HALF

1

The new words in each lesson are placed in the margin. Phonetic words are placed below each lesson.

See my doll.   see
                                                          my
                                                         doll

2

See my new doll.   new

     dew   mew   few   pew

3

I have a new doll.   have
I have a big doll.   big

     dig   jig   fig   pig   wig

4

Sue has a doll.   Sue
Sue has a cat.   has
                                                          cat

     fat   hat   mat   rat   bat   sat

Four lessons constitute a week's work. Review on Friday.

5

See this girl.   this
She has a cat.   girl
                                        she

6

Sue is a good girl.   is
She has a doll.   good

        wood   hood

7

I see a good boy.   boy
Sam is a good boy.   Sam

   joy   toy   dam   jam   ham   ram

8

I see a cat and a doll.   and
Sam has the cat.   the

At the close of the second, and every succeeding week, review not only the new words, but also difficult words of previous weeks.

9

See this ball.   ball
It is my ball.   it

   fall   call   hall   tall   wall

10

I have a big red ball.   red
Sam and I play ball.   play

   bed   fed   led   Ned   wed

11

I like to play ball.   like
Sam likes to play ball.   to

12

This is my new ball.   can
Sam and I can play with it.   with

    Dan   fan   man   pan   ran   tan

13

Sue has a bird.   bird
It can call and sing.   sing

    king   ring   wing

14

Sue can sing and play.   does
Sam does not like to sing.   not

    dot   got   hot   lot   pot   rot

Second Year—First Half

15

I have a pet bird.
It can sing you a song.

   pet
   you
   song

bet	let	net	wet
get	met	set	long

16

That bird has a nest.
It is in the wood.

   that
   nest
   in

best pest rest test vest west

17

The cow gives milk.
Sue does not like milk.

   cow
   gives
   milk

now vow silk

18

The cow eats hay.
Ned fed the cow and the pig.

   eats
   hay

day	lay	pay	way
gay	may	ray	say

19

See the red cow.
She loves her calf.

   loves
   her
   calf

half

Write a sentence about the cow. End it with a period.

Second Year — First Half

20

See the old cow.   old
Dan is kind to her.   kind

    bind   find   mind   rind

21

I have a dog and a cat.   dog
The dog can run and play.   run

    fog   log   bun   gun
    hog   jog   fun   sun

22

I love my pet dog.   me
See me pat him.   him

23

I call my dog Jack.   Jack
I like the name of Jack.   name
                                                                             of

    back   pack   came   lame
    rack   tack   game   same

Second Year — First Half

24
The cat can lap milk.   lap
Jack laps milk, too.   too

    cap   map   nap   rap   sap   tap

25
Ned has a sled.   sled
He has fun with it.   he

    bed   fed   led   Ned   red   wed

26
The snow is soft.   snow
My cap fell in the snow.   soft
                                             fell

    bell   cell   Nell   sell   tell   well

27
The dog likes the snow.   for
It is fun for him to roll in it.   roll

                      nor

28
All boys like the snow.   all
They like ice, too.   they
                                             ice

29
Snow keeps the roots warm.   keeps
Nell does not like the snow.   roots
                                             warm

                      boots

Second Year — First Half

30

The bean is a seed.   bean
You can eat this seed.   seed

    deed   feed   heed   need   reed   weed

31

We can eat roots, too.   we
We eat the beet.   beet

        feet   meet

32

The red beets are ripe.   are
May does not like them.   ripe
                                                                           them

        pipe   wipe

33

The sun has set.   will
Now my bird will sing very low.   ver'y
                                                                    low

        bill   hill   mill   rill
        fill   kill   pill   sill

34

That is the last bell.   last
Now Jack must run.   must

     fast   mast   past   dust   just   rust

35

Anna can not find her new hat.   An'na
She does not like to be late.   be
                                               late

     date   fate   gate   Kate   mate   rate

36

I have a nut and a date.   nut
The date has a pit.   pit

     cut   but   rut   bit   fit   hit   lit

37

That bird has two wings.   two
She can fly to her nest.   fly

                     sly

38

My bird has sand in his cage.   sand
I feed seeds to my bird.   his
                                               cage

        band   hand   land

39

The ice is thin.   thin
We must not step on it.   step
                                               on

Second Year — First Half

40

Here is Ned in the snow.   here
The snow is cold and wet.   cold

    bold   fold   gold   hold   sold   told

41

The old hen is here.   hen
She has left her nest.   left

    Ben   den   men   ten   pen

42

This hen laid an egg.   laid
We must try to feed her now.   egg
                                                    try

    maid   paid   raid   cry   dry   fry

43

Fill the cup with milk.   cup
Our cat and dog like milk.   our

Second Year — First Half

44

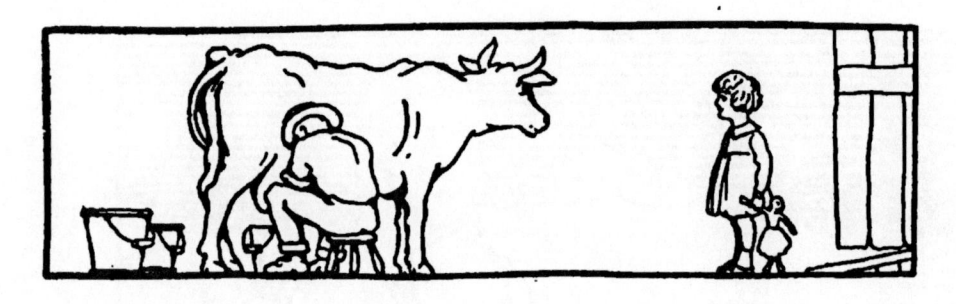

The cow gave a pail of milk.   gave
I saw her give it.   pail
     saw

    cave   Dave   pave   rave   save   wave
    bail   fail   jail   mail   nail   rail

45

I saw the bird in the tree.   tree
I must not hit the poor bird.   poor

     free

46

Ben does not run or jump.   or
He is too lame.   jump

     bump   dump   lump   pump

47

Ned goes for the mail.   goes
He must walk fast.   walk

     talk

Second Year — First Half

48

You saw me stop and play ball with Ned.　　stop
I did not play very well.　　　　　　　　　did

    bid　　　hid　　　kid　　　lid　　　rid

49

We saw a big rat.　　　　　　　　　　　in'to
It ran into a hole and hid.　　　　　　　hole

50

Puss saw the rat.　　　　　　　　　　　Puss
Puss has nice soft feet.　　　　　　　　nice

    dice　　　mice　　　rice　　　vice

51

I saw Puss play with the rat.　　　　　then
Then she ate it.　　　　　　　　　　　ate

52

Puss does not want the rat.　　　　　　want
She has too much to eat.　　　　　　　much

             such

53

John hid in the hay.　　　　　　　　　John
Anna saw him hide there.　　　　　　　hide
　　　　　　　　　　　　　　　　　　there

    bide　　ride　　side　　tide　　wide

54

Ned had a red cap.   had
It was too big for him.   was

    bad   lad   mad   sad

55

Mary made a new hat.   Ma′ry
It was too big, too.   made

    fade   wade

56

Ruth saw the sun rise.   Ruth
It was like a big red ball.   rise

57

I saw the moon rise.   moon
It was up in the sky.   up
                    sky

    loon   noon   soon

58

The stars were near the moon.   stars
The sun had set.   were
                    near

    dear   fear   hear   rear   year

59

See the fish in the pond.   fish
I see a duck, too.   pond
                  duck

    dish   wish   bond   fond

Second Year — First Half

60

That box is made of tin.
Ned told me so.

    bin   fin   pin   sin   win   fox

box
tin
so

61

Ruth must go home now.
Her doll fell into the mud.

    bud   cud

go
home
mud

62

Anna will make a cake.
I hope it will be good.

    bake   lake   sake   wake   Pope
    cake   rake   take   mope   rope

make
hope

63

The flag is on the pole.
It is a fine big flag.

    dine   line   mine   nine   pine   vine

flag
fine

64

The boat is a big one.
It will sail out with the tide.

    coat   goat

boat
one
out

Drill. Put the following words on the blackboard, and have pupils underline the small word included in each: *cat, Sam, ball, play, sled, late, cold, sand, seed, song, made, hope, near, coat, there, sing, nice.*

SECOND YEAR — SECOND HALF

1

I am in a new class. I must begin the term well.

    bass   mass   pass   glass   brass   grass

class
be gin'
term

2

We have a big horse. My brother and I feed him sugar.

horse
broth'er
sug'ar

3

Kate goes to the store. She gets bread and butter.

    bore   core   more   pore   sore   tore

store
bread
but'ter

4

Do you love the baby? Then kiss her.

    hiss   miss   bliss

do
ba'by
kiss

Second Year — Second Half

REVIEW

Anna	Ruth	goes	cow	hear	met
John	bird	name	girl	meet	song

With each preceding lesson study 3 review words. Devote Friday to a general review, giving no new work.

5

My father keeps his horse very clean. He feeds him well, every day.

fa′ther
clean
ev′er y

    bean   lean   mean

6

Our horse eats hay and oats. He eats grass and apples when he can get them.

oats
ap′ples
when

7

Do not drive Dick too fast. You will hurt him.

drive
Dick
hurt

  kick lick nick pick sick wick
        dive five hive

8

John has a pony and a cart. He bought them from my father.

po′ny
cart
bought
from

    dart part tart

Write a question about Dick. Put the proper mark at the end.

Review

Jack	Sue	dish	egg	west	walk
Mary	such	hide	poor	tide	nice

9

The robin came north in the spring. He made his nest in the old apple tree.

rob″in
north
spring

forth   king   sing   ring   wing

10

The nest was made of mud and straw. Mrs. Robin laid four blue eggs.

straw
four
blue

pour   glue

11

The father robin gets food for the baby robins. Robins like worms and fruit.

food
worms
fruit

12

Did you see the young robin eat the cherry? The farmer does not like the robin.

young
cher′ry
farm′er

Review

pond	soft	near	silk	made	left
snow	old	roll	pipe	coat	sing

Why are Jack, Mary, and Sue called *given* names? Write all the given names that you can spell.

13

Half of these grapes are green. Do not eat such fruit.

these
grapes
green

keen   seen

14

I have a bright new cent. I can buy an apple.

bright
cent
buy

fight   might   right   tight   lent   tent
light   night   sight   dent   sent   went

15

Next Friday I shall go out in my new boat. Will mother let you go, too?

next
Fri'day
shall
moth'er

text

16

The milkman has a gallon of milk. Shall I buy a pint or a quart?

gal'lon
pint
quart

c

Review

| very | need | out | tree | sky | want |
| take | like | sake | most | wipe | talk |

17

My thick coat is made of wool. We get wool from the sheep.

wool
sheep
thick

| deep | peep | brick | click |
| keep | weep | chick | stick |

18

The wool is cut off in the spring, before it is too hot. The wool is soft and white.

off
be fore′
white

19

A young sheep is called a lamb. We eat the flesh of sheep and lambs.

called
lamb
flesh

fresh

20

The man who tends the sheep has a dog to help him. The sheep dog knows all the sheep and lambs.

who
tends
help
knows

| bend | lend | mend | send |

Write a sentence about a sheep, and end it with a period. Write a sentence about a lamb, and end it with a question mark.

Second Year — Second Half

REVIEW

lame	rope	save	wake	roots	try
find	make	game	there	mine	year

21

In January and February we have snow and ice. We have rain, too.

Jan'u a ry
Feb'ru a ry
rain

gain　　main　　pain　　vain　　chain
　　drain　　grain　　stain　　train

22

See the black clouds in the west. I am afraid it will rain soon.

black
clouds
a fraid'

23

The rain which keeps me from my play, makes the grass grow. Can you catch the rain drops?

which
grow
catch
drops

snatch　　hatch　　latch　・ match　　patch

24

The baby can not use a fork or spoon. We feed her milk every day.

use
fork
spoon

cork　　　　　　pork

REVIEW

flag	nest	they	mice	rake	paid
land	wave	half	dry	stop	hand

Write all words that end with *ame*.

25

Last Saturday I saw a deer in the park. He was eating grass.

    bark   dark   hark   lark   mark

Sat'ur day
deer
park

26

The deer is reddish brown. He feeds on grass, leaves, and moss.

    loss   boss   toss   across   floss   moss

red'dish
brown
leaves

27

Did you ever see a deer run to cover? He runs and jumps with a swift light step.

ev'er
cov'er
swift

28

The horns of the deer are called antlers. A young deer is called a fawn.

    born   corn   torn   worn   dawn   lawn

horns
ant'lers
fawn

Second Year — Second Half

Review

Kate	play	warm	ate	left	pave
sled	stars	told	fold	tree	loves

29

May we play on the lawn till dark?
You may if you go home before six or seven
in the evening.

     fix   mix

six
sev′en
e′ven ing

30

In December the days are very short.
We have supper after dark.

   fort port sort

De cem′ber
short
sup′per
aft′er

31

In school we use paper and pencil. We
must keep all papers clean.

school
pa′per
pen′cil

32

Our long days are in June. I often dig in
my garden till six or seven at night.

      tune

June
oft′en
gar′den

Review

fear	seed	rest	wing	fly	fish
jump	soon	last	was	good	boat

Mark the silent letters in *often, boat, fear*.

33

We should give all plants sun and light. They need water, too.

       could   would

should
plants
wa′ter

34

The sheep carries seeds from place to place in its wool. The wind carries seeds from place to place, too.

    brace   Grace   trace

car′ries
place
its
wind

35

Do you know what we call the fruit of the oak tree? It is called an acorn.

what
oak
a′corn

Second Year — Second Half

36

In October the oak leaves turn red and brown and yellow. Dick and I keep them off the lawn.

Oc to'ber
turn
yel'low

burn   churn   bellow   fellow   mellow

Review

cake	much	our	ripe	mind	dust
boat	goat	fast	must	sold	eats

37

Whose watch is this? I think it is mine, as I bought one last Saturday.

whose
watch
think

link   mink   pink   rink   sink   wink

38

I must study every lesson before I go out to play. Does your brother study at night?

stud'y
les'son
your

39

Next Tuesday I am going out to lunch and to supper. I shall take my sister with me.

Tues'day
lunch
sis'ter

bunch   punch   munch

Write all the words on this page that have two or three syllables.

40

Kate made the dress which was worn by the poor child. I think she did it last November.

       bless   cress   tress

dress
child
No vem'ber

Review

| king | rear | tall | cage | past | gave |
| lake | tame | moon | line | free | step |

41

Sister and I call our dog Sport. His brown hair is soft and curly.

       fair   pair   chair

sport
hair
cur'ly

42

The dog has soft pads on his feet, like the cat. Can the dog pull in his claws and hide them?

       bull   full

pads
pull
claws

43

Dogs eat meat and lap milk. Their teeth are very sharp.

    beat   heat   neat   peat   seat

meat
their
teeth
sharp

44

It is queer that the black spot in the eye of the cat grows wide in the dark. The dog has eyes that do not change.

queer
eye
change

Review

| date | dew | pole | feed | pump | mail |
| cry | ice | ring | nine | fade | one |

45

Mr. and Mrs. White will stay in the city till next April. Then they will go to see their son.

    pity

stay
cit'y
A'pril
son

46

Every summer I go out of the city in July and August. Is it very hot in the city in summer?

sum'mer
Ju ly'
Au'gust

Underline the small word in each of the following: *meat, date, son, eat, hair, think, your, seat, carry, plant, what, acorn, pencil, garden, antler.*

47

You must look at the pretty blue hat which papa bought me. The baby tore my old one.

look
pret'ty
pa pa'

book   cook   hook   took   brook   shook

48

There were three girls in the yard. They were busy with their lessons.

three
yard
bus'y

card   hard   lard

Review

| bean | calf | pen | deed | late | side |
| dear | pill | sail | gives | rises | boots |

49

Last Wednesday I found the nest of an owl. It was in an old tree.

Wednes'day
found
owl

bound   mound   pound   round   sound

50

In the nest which I found, were four little eggs. Shall I show them to you some day?

    blow   glow   crow   snow
    flow   slow   grow   come

lit′tle
show
some

51

Some owls are gray and some are white. They never make much noise when they fly.

gray
nev′er
noise

52

The claws of the owl are very strong. He eats both mice and small birds.

    fall   call   hall   tall   wall   stall

strong
both
small

Review

| cold | sand | came | rice | fail | gate |
| pine | vest | duck | just | long | kill |

53

How much money have you? I have ten dollars, five cents, and a dime. What sum have I?

mon'ey
dol'lars
dime
sum

    lime   time   honey

54

Fred takes a lesson every Monday and Wednesday. Do you take lessons on those days too?

Fred
Mon'day
those

bed	led	red	sled	fled
fed	Ned	wed	bled	shed

55

How much salt did you put in the soup? Come here and I shall show you.

salt
put
soup

    halt   malt

56

Please open the door. I want to take a peep at the snow. Now I can make some snowballs.

please
o'pen
door

Review

rust	weed	laid	bold	saw	best
fate	few	same	home	pin	fog

Make, from the words on this page, a list of words that have letters doubled.

57

May I go with you next Thursday to see the beaver dams? Henry and I were there last Monday, and saw eight.

Thurs′day
bea′ver
Hen′ry
eight

58

The beavers build these dams so that the door of their house will be under water. Did you ever see a beaver dam?

build
house
un′der

grouse   mouse

59

Mr. Beaver does not make or mend his house or dam until September. I am sure he wants the coat of mud to freeze very hard.

Sep tem′ber
sure
freeze

pure   cure

60

Can the beavers cut down big trees? Yes, it is true that they do this with their teeth.

down
yes
true

gown   town

Review

feet	wide	band	hate	hold	beet
bake	tail	sly	here	wish	fond

61

We get silk from the tiny silkworm. It feeds on the leaf of the mulberry tree. It eats every leaf it can find.

ti'ny
leaf
mul'ber ry

62

Then it spins a little ball of silk around its body and goes to sleep. Did you ever see any of these balls of silk?

spins
a round'
bod'y
an'y

bin	fin	sin	chin
din	pin	tin	thin

63

In March, April, May, and June the farmer is very busy. There are a dozen things to be done.

March
doz'en
things
done

64

Every Sunday I go to see my aunt. I like to take dinner with her.

Sun'day
aunt
din'ner

THIRD YEAR — FIRST HALF

1

The children who did not study their lessons last term are sorry now. Are you one of these lazy children?

    hazy   crazy

chil′dren
sor′ry
la′zy

2

Do you want a flower in the school room? Then you must plant some seeds in a pot of earth.

    loom   gloom   bloom   broom

flow′er
room
earth

3

Every plant has root, stem, and leaves. Most plants also have flowers, fruit, and seeds. Can you find each part?

stem
most
al′so
each

4

I always help my mother before I come to   al′ways
school. As soon as I reach home, I help her   reach
again.   a gain′

     beach   peach   teach   bleach

Review

afraid	meat	Wednesday	want	child
cherry	pretty	walk	lame	lamb
keeps	goes	eats	apples	mend

With each preceding lesson take 3 or 4 review words, so that when Lesson 4 is taught, these review words will also be finished.

5

Every Monday morning we begin a new   morn′ing
week. We must learn each lesson well.   week
   learn

     leek   peek   seek   cheek   creek

6

September, October, and November are the   au′tumn
three autumn months. The leaves of the   months
maple turn red and yellow and brown.   ma′ple

NOTE TO TEACHER. — Frequently have pupils make an alphabetical list of words on a page. In this grade alphabetical order refers to the first letter only.

7

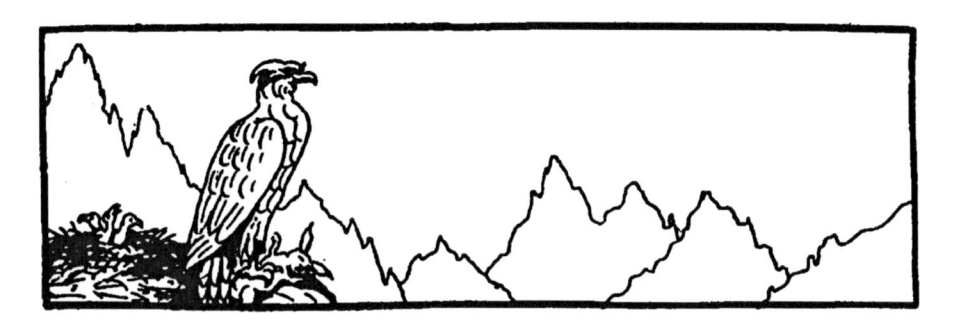

The eagle feeds on rabbits, small birds, and fish. He builds his nest in a high place.

ea′gle
rab′bits
high

nigh   sigh

8

We can see an eagle on every quarter and fifty cent piece. On what other piece do we find the eagle?

quar′ter
fif′ty
piece

Review

pure	lake	grapes	study	warm
strong	April	might	white	cage
try	class	quart	left	wish

9

Do you drink coffee for your breakfast? I am sure that milk is much better for children.

drink
cof′fee
break′fast
bet′ter

fetter   letter   setter   wetter

10

Please bring me the orange which is on the table. I bought it for my dinner and paid two cents for it.

bring
or'ange
ta'ble

11

The fruit is that part of the plant which holds the seeds. The ugly bur that sticks to our clothes is the fruit of a plant.

ug'ly
bur
clothes

cur　　　　fur

12

Dogs and sheep carry these seed cases from place to place. I know seeds which are carried away by wind and water.

car'ry
ca'ses
a way'

Harry　　　marry

Review

around	queer	August	weed
clean	sugar	green	like
grass	eight	money	west
Monday	made	loves	please

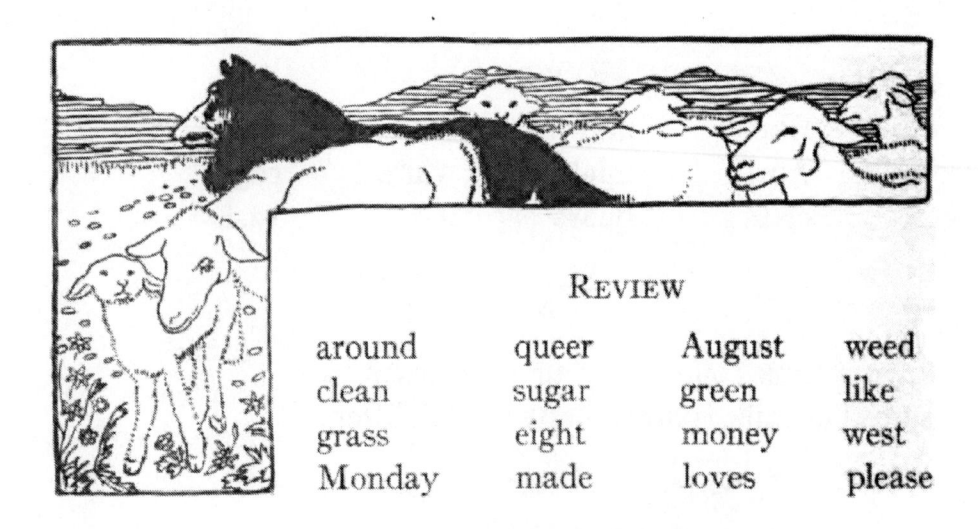

13

The butcher and the baker call at our house every Tuesday, Thursday, and Saturday. Julia buys meat and bread for our dinner.

butch′er
ba′ker
Ju′li a

      maker   shaker

14

I like to play with Grace's doll very much. It can lie down, shut its eyes, and go to sleep. Can you guess its name?

lie
shut
sleep
guess

   die   tie   but   cut   hut   rut

15

My mother and sister have been away from home since Wednesday, and we shall be happy to see them once more.

been
since
hap′py
once

16

We feed Anna's canary every day at eleven or twelve o'clock. He likes all kinds of seeds and fruit.

ca na′ry
e lev′en
twelve

Review

aunt	mother	wool	wore	wide
cover	rain	right	milk	year
grow	summer	Sunday	tail	wipe

17

When my father was sick, we called a doctor who lives in New York. Dr. Black said that father must have rest and sleep.

doc′tor
New York′
said

18

As Julia's house was a mile away, I took the car at First Street. I did not get the right one, and so I was not on time.

mile
car
first
street

    bar   far   jar   tar

19

Helen gave a party to thirty little boys and girls. They had cakes and ices and many nice things to eat.

Hel′en
par′ty
thir′ty

Third Year — First Half

20

When Jack hurt his finger, he could not help his father. He was such a good boy that his sister told him a story almost every day.

fin'ger
sto'ry
al'most

REVIEW

baby	mouse	worn	curly	swift
cross	robin	name	hatch	yard
hair	supper	begin	round	near

21

When I go into our parlor I can hear the clock tick. My mother will not let me touch this clock. Father winds it every eighth day.

par'lor
clock
touch
eighth

    dock   lock   mock   rock   sock
      flock   frock   shock   stock

22

My father gave my brother and me silver pencils. Fred's pencil was soon broken, but I kept mine a month.

sil'ver
bro'ken
kept

23

How many inches are there in a foot, George? There are twelve inches in a foot, and three feet in a yard.

in'ches
foot
George

24

December, January, and February are the winter months. We have many storms, but just at this time we also have skating.

win′ter
storms
skat′ing

Review

December	Saturday	need	Henry	term
heat	teeth	black	next	young
never	yellow	deer	school	our

25

Does John go out early in the morning? Yes, he wahts to earn money to buy a big chair for his mama.

ear′ly
earn
ma ma′

26

The fox and the wolf are about as large as dogs. Their teeth are very sharp, as they are made to tear their food.

wolf
a bout′
large
tear

27

The nose of the wolf and the nose of the fox are more pointed than a dog's nose. Their tails are much more bushy.

nose
point'ed
bush'y

hose   rose

28

The puppies do not open their eyes till they are between ten and twelve days old. They are twice as fond of play as a dog's puppies.

pup'pies
be tween'
twice

REVIEW

deep	seat	paid	house	things
horse	thick	blue	north	boat
noise	bird	dinner	September	pail

29

I am sure that the boys and girls who add and spell well, are the ones whose work is always good.

add
spell
work

30

There are three classes of bees. They all live together in a hive and feed on honey, which they collect in the summer.

bees
to geth'er
col lect'

Put the following words in sentences: *bushy, twice, collect.*

31

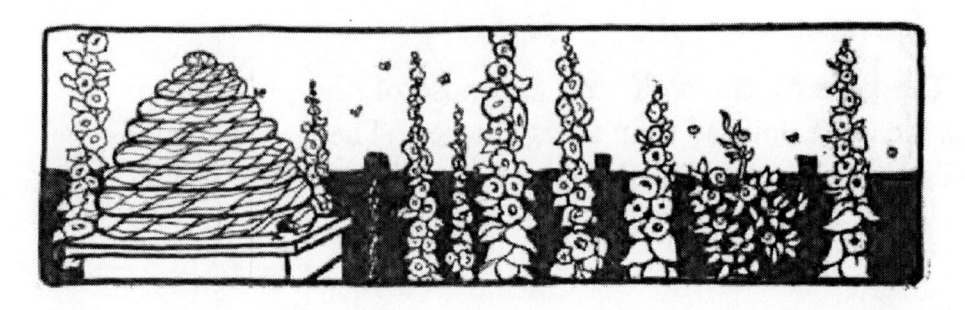

The queen bee lays the eggs. The drones do no work and have no sting.

queen
drones
sting

spring   bring   thing   cling   fling

32

The workers get food for the entire hive. They get this honey from the flowers. They like clover very much.

work′ers
en tire′
clo′ver

Review

body	November	boots	dozen	sharp
dollars	seven	play	January	three
hurt	think	book	oak	cake

33

Friday noon I went to the grocery store and bought a large squash and a quart of pears. My mother cooked them for dinner on Sunday.

gro′cer y
squash
pears

34

While mother was busy, I read to my little sister under the old elm tree. Did you ever try to keep a little sister quiet?

while
read
elm
qui′et

35

Do you read word by word? If you do, read a page a day, for a month, and you will soon improve.

word
page
im prove′

    cage   rage   sage   wage   stage

36

The wind o' the West
I love it best.
The wind o' the East
I love it least.

east
least

Review

dress	sheep	rear	July	tiny
June	Thursday	bought	October	dear
oats	coat	eye	shook	roots

37

The wind o' the South
Has sweet in its mouth.
The wind o' the North
Sends great storms forth.
    — Margaret Sangster.

south
sweet
mouth
great

38

When we raise plants, we must take care of them. They need sun and air and water. In March some of them may begin to bloom.

    bare   dare   fare   hare   pare   rare

raise
care
air

39

Last Saturday I saw twenty merry children on their way to the park. Can you tell me why they were so happy?

    berry   ferry   cherry

twen'ty
mer'ry
why

40

Do not ask me to go to the floor above this one. I did not know how I could reach this floor.

ask
floor
a bove'

Review

bread	often	dish	father	show
farmer	short	sail	know	fear
keep	took	brick	open	sake

Third Year — First Half

41

Children, sing to Him whose care
Makes the land so rich and fair;
Raise your tuneful voices high
To our Father in the sky.
— Margaret Sangster.

rich
tune'ful
voi'ces

42

Frogs lay their eggs in a kind of jelly. It takes about a month to hatch these eggs. Then we see the tadpole.

frogs
jel'ly
tad'pole

43

A tadpole is all head and tail. Did you ever watch the gills disappear and the legs grow?

dead

head
gills
dis ap pear'

44

As the legs of the tadpole grow, the tail disappears. Then we have the perfect little frog, that feeds on several insects.

per'fect
sev'er al
in'sects

Review

bright	pain	feet	flesh	sight
February	sick	save	latch	town
lamb	torn	brother	pair	seed

45

Children, sing to One whose love
Broods your merry days above;   broods
Lift your tuneful voices high   lift
To our Father in the sky.
    — Margaret Sangster.

 gift sift drift swift

46

Everything else one can turn and turn about,   else
and make old look like new, but there's no   coax'ing
coaxing boots and shoes to look better than   shoes
they are. — George Eliot.   than

47

I don't like the cold days of winter. Jack   frost
Frost bites my fingers and my toes. I like   bites
April and May much better.   toes

 foes woes cost lost

Third Year — First Half

48

Nearly every day the rose's pretty face was washed by the dew. Was the dear little flower happy when it felt the drops of dew?

near'ly
face
washed
felt

lace   mace   pace   race   belt   melt

Review

brown	sister	silk	leave	trick
leaf	train	build	paper	free
papa	flag	found	snatch	sky

49

Said young Dandelion
With a sweet air,
"I have my eye on
Miss Daisy fair."
— Miss Mulock.

dan'de li on
dai'sy

50

Don't you see those black clouds coming up in the west? I think it will rain in fifteen or twenty minutes.

com'ing
fif'teen
min'utes

51

I tried to drive my uncle's big black horse to the barn. I soon found I could not whip him.

tried
un'cle
barn
whip

      cried   dried   fried

52

Isn't it too early to light the lamp? No, I wish to write a letter, and it must be done by nine o'clock to-night.

lamp
write
o'clock'
to-night'

| camp | damp | cramp | tramp | stamp |

Review

busy	patch	gate	freeze	sore
fork	small	snow	die	Tuesday
lesson	true	butter	pencil	girl

53

In winter I get up at night
And dress by yellow candle light.
In summer, quite the other way,
I have to go to bed by day.
    — R. L. Stevenson.[1]

can'dle
quite
oth'er

handle

54

I wish you'd not forget to speak to your uncle to-day about the fruit which I bought for him. I have grapes, peaches, and pears.

for get'
speak
to-day'

| leak | weak | creak | sneak | freak |

Write three things that are yellow. Write at least three words that end with *ow*.

[1] From "Poems and Ballads," copyright, 1895, 1896, by Charles Scribner's Sons.

55

The sparrow's eggs are speckled. She lays five or six. They hatch in sixteen or seventeen days. Did you ever see one?

spar′row
speck′led
six′teen
sev′en teen

56

The mother bird only feeds her young ones for a week. Then they must pick up their own food from the ground, or wherever they can find it.

on′ly
ground
wher ev′er

Review

called	pint	stars	lunch	under
fresh	sound	carries	pity	hear
little	turn	Friday	soup	take

57

Nay, only look what I have found!
A sparrow's nest upon the ground.
A sparrow's nest, as you may see,
Blown out of yonder old elm tree.
— Mary Howitt.

nay
blown
yon′der

58

Here are eighteen lemons to make a cool drink for the children. Are they coming on Tuesday or Wednesday?

    fool   pool   tool   spool   stool

eight een'
lem'ons
cool

59

Didn't Harry break his arm some time ago? His mother told me he cried with the pain.

break
arm
a go'

60

When I pull the string, the kitten follows it from place to place. She likes to jump up in the air for it, too.

    bitten   mitten

string
kit'ten
fol'lows

Review

catch	please	here	gallon	spring
fruit	spoon	talk	March	vain
main	use	cent	pony	home

61

In the summer months, June, July, and August, we use very little coal. Sometimes we get a bushel, which the grocer sends in a bag.

    lag   rag   sag   tag   goal

coal
bush'el
gro'cer
bag

62

How many eggs does your sister Emma get for a quarter? I bought fourteen the other day, at our own grocer's.

Em'ma
four'teen
own

63

The lily grew under glass till we could put it with the other flowers. We want it as a gift for Aunt Ellen, who will soon be seventy years old.

lil'y
grew
El'len
sev'en ty

    blew   crew   chew   stew   drew   flew

64

At home I have my own soap, brush, and comb. When I go away in summer, I always take them with me.

soap
brush
comb

Review

chair	pound	just	eight	store
garden	stay	true	mean	water
match	watch	change	pour	tree

Third Year — First Half

NOTE TO TEACHER. — The ready recognition of the component parts of words is a great aid in spelling. This can be begun by requiring children to write in a column the small words they find in the following list.

forget	woodwork	playmate	daybreak
milkman	bulldog	sunrise	milkmaid
bedroom	butterfly	sunset	bluefish
anything	snowdrop	schoolboy	bullfrog
bandage	daylight	workroom	boatman
Sunday	oatmeal	gooseberry	sunbeam

Form new words by combining a word in the 1st or 2d column with a word in the 3d or 4th column.

band	day	cup	paper
school	foot	room	shine
sun	flax	thing	time
play	news	step	cap
butter	night	seed	box

NOTE TO TEACHER. — To pronounce the following words correctly requires frequent practice. Children should not only say them singly, but should use each one in a very simple sentence.

just	height	chocolate	toward
voice	injure	drawing	window
once	introduce	deaf	whether
singing	length	dew	which
catch	library	drowned	whistle
this	mischief	engine	yeast
that	museum	figure	forehead
new	again	recess	umbrella

Third Year — First Half

Hartford, Nov. 30, 1915.

Dear Marion,

You do not know how I miss you, because now I have only Edna to play with. Do you think your mother would let you make us a visit at Christmas time? Please ask her, and let me know as soon as you can.

Your loving friend,
Alice Baker.

Boston, Dec. 10, 1915.

Dear Alice,

When the postman gave me your letter, I just jumped for joy. Mother says I may go to Hartford the day after Christmas. Father is going to New York then, and he will take me. I know you will meet me, as I can hardly wait to see you.

Your loving friend,
Marion.

THIRD YEAR — SECOND HALF

1

Alice is a gentle loving child. She has a kind heart, and always does her very best to please both father and mother.

Al′ice
gen′tle
lov′ing
heart

2

How much time he gains, who does not look to see what his neighbor says or does or thinks, but only at what he does himself, to make it just and holy. — MARCUS AURELIUS.

neigh′bor
says
him self′
ho′ly

3

I cannot stay the east wind
Or thaw its icy smart;
But I can keep a corner warm
In mother's loving heart.
— *Teachers' Magazine.*

thaw
i′cy
smart
cor′ner

Third Year — Second Half

4

Have you ever seen an ostrich? Yes, my cousin and I saw some of these big birds yesterday in Central Park. They are very strong and can run fast.

os'trich
cous'in
yes'ter day
cen'tral

Review

autumn	perfect	hurt	lesson	aunt
daisy	table	sister	piece	January
honey	around	always	teach	sound

5

When I am grown to man's estate
I shall be very proud and great,
And tell the other girls and boys
Not to meddle with my toys.
— Stevenson.

grown
es tate'
proud
med'dle

6

Among the flowers sent to church were nineteen or twenty lilies. We've never before seen such pretty white ones.

a mong'
church
nine'teen
lil'ies

7

Some of grandma's friends took a long journey to see her on her seventy-ninth birthday. Did Emma show you the fruit which the children gave to grandma?

grand'ma
friends
jour'ney
ninth
birth'day

8

The butterfly only lives for one summer. It does not fly at night. It goes to its resting place about five o'clock in the afternoon. I caught one to-day.

but'ter fly
rest'ing
aft er noon'
caught

REVIEW

also	quarter	soup	insects	bought
dead	tear	baker	quiet	July
inches	black	disappear	than	sugar

9

All things whatsoever ye would that men should do to you, do ye even so to them, for this is the law and the prophets.
— *The Bible.*

what so ev'er
e'ven
law
proph'ets

10

From breakfast on through all the day
At home among my friends I stay,
But every night I go abroad
Afar into the land of Nod.
— STEVENSON.

through
a broad'
a far'
nod.

Third Year — Second Half

11

I learned to add and subtract very well, but I cannot multiply and divide as easily. I spent November, December, and January trying to learn.

sub tract'
mul'ti ply
di vide'
eas'i ly
spent

12

You've been out to gather wild flowers, I am sure. Did you climb the rocks for them, or did you find them near the river?

gath'er
wild
climb
riv'er

Review

beach	quite	bread	Julia	brother
dried	thirty	summer	rabbit	lamb
jelly	know	berry	to-day	Sunday

13

I love little Pussy,
Her coat is so warm;
And if I don't hurt her,
She'll do me no harm.
So I'll not pull her tail,
Nor drive her away,
But Pussy and I
Very gently will play.
— Jane Taylor.

Pus'sy
harm
gen'tly

Write abbreviations for any words on this page.

14

Frank's father sent him one hundred and fifty dollars for Christmas. What do you think he will do with that amount of money? He may go home for the twelfth of February.

Frank
hun′dred
Christ′mas
a mount′
twelfth

15

My rabbit likes to run in the field. When I feed him carrots or tender cabbage leaves, he looks at me as if he would like to say, "Thank you."

field
car′rots
ten′der
cab′bage
thank

16

The earthworm bores through the soil and softens it. Then the rain can reach the roots of plants, and also any seeds which happen to be in the ground.

earth′worm
soil
sof′tens
hap′pen

Review

better	raise	leaf	eagle	busy
each	toes	thick	fifth	lie
kept	build	between	together	think

17

Only a tender flower
Sent to us to rear;
Only a life to love
While we are here.
Only a baby small,
Never at rest,
Small, but how dear to us,
God knoweth best.
— MATTHIAS BARR.

life
God
know′eth

18

When our donkey came to a bridge which he did not like to cross, he always fell into the river. To cure him of the trick, we once made him carry two baskets of sponges. This day he found it was a mistake to fall into the water.

don′key
bridge
bas′kets
spon′ges
mis take′

19

What did you see in the country? I saw a number of things, but I liked the lovely flowers best of all. One day I picked an apron full before six o'clock in the morning.

coun′try
num′ber
love′ly
a′pron

20

Woodpeckers have a strong bill, so they can bore for insects. The farmer does not like these birds, because they sample his best fruit and often hammer his trees full of holes.

wood'peck er
be cause'
sam'ple
ham'mer

Review

maid	blew	read	March	earth
came	early	to-night	Thursday	lazy
warm	large	carries	break	said

21

Bright little dandelion,
Downy, yellow face,
Peeping up among the grass
With such gentle grace;
Minding not the April wind,
Blowing rude and cold,
Brave little dandelion,
With a heart of gold.
    — From *McMurray's Classic Stories.*

down'y
blow'ing
rude
brave

22

Dr. White and his wife spent Easter week at the seashore. Their home is in Boston, but they do not live there during June, July, or August. They always leave the city about the twenty-fifth of May.

wife
East'er
sea'shore
Bos'ton
dur'ing

23

Does Ruth's music teacher let her play by ear? No, she does not, because she wishes Ruth to profit by her lessons and to play every piece as it is written.

mu′sic
teach′er
ear
prof′it
writ′ten

24

All parents like to have people praise their children. They like to feel that their children never forget to be polite.

par′ents
peo′ple
praise
po lite′

REVIEW

paid	touch	train	eighteen	cherry
eats	chair	breakfast	seventeen	Monday
year	meat	learn	tried	true

25

When the smaller child saw the lady, she did not know she was a fairy and said, "Do you think I shall give you a drink from this silver pitcher?"

small′er
la′dy
fair′y
pitch′er

26

Last Friday night mama said with a smile, "Sarah, have you studied your lessons for next week? Eight o'clock Monday morning must find you ready for school."

smile
Sa′rah
stud′ied
read′y

27

One day in September my sister's hus-   hus′band
band wrote me a letter, saying, "We expect   wrote
to come to Chicago in October and hope   ex pect′
you will not go away until we have seen   Chi ca′go
you."   un til′

28

The teacher said to her class, "When   ex am′ple
you work an example in division, be sure   di vi′sion
that the remainder is smaller than the   re main′der
divisor."   di vi′sor

REVIEW

broken	several	Tuesday	want	clean
eleven	twelve	sail	loves	money
lemons	mother	lame	twenty	watch

29

The robin and the bluebird
Soon after flew away,
But as they left the treetop   blue′bird
I think I heard them say,   tree′top
"If birds and flowers have work to do,   heard
Why, so have little children too."
— HELEN C. BACON.

Select from your reader five sentences, each containing a direct quotation.

30

James cried, "Whose candy is this, lying on the shelf?" As no one said a word, he ate it.

James
can'dy
ly'ing
shelf

31

Any child who wants to become strong and healthy, must have plenty of sunshine. How much time do you spend in the air each day?

be come'
health'y
plen'ty
sun'shine
spend

32

On the tenth of February, Mr. and Mrs. Mason went to Cuba to visit people who lived there the entire year. The doctor said that the change would be good for Mr. Mason, who was slightly ill.

tenth
ma'son
Cu'ba
vis'it
slight'ly

Review

broom	shoes	noise	entire	tail
Ellen	twice	water	lily	walk
letter	cover	brush	sigh	game

33

What, green leaves! Have you fingers?
Then the maple laughed with glee.
Yes, just as many as you have;
Count them and you shall see.
— *Teachers' Magazine.*

laughed
glee
count

34

A hungry fox saw some grapes on a vine. He sprang up and tried to get them. Finding them beyond his reach, he said, "Just as I thought. Those grapes are sour."

hun′gry
sprang
be yond′
thought
sour

35

The fairies danced till dawn, and then they hid under the petals of the flowers. If we look, perhaps we may see them when we go to the woods next Friday.

fair′ies
danced
pet′als
per haps′

36

Our family is so very large that we eat a loaf of bread at each meal. Can you tell me how many loaves we shall use this month?

fam′i ly
meal
loaf
loaves

Review

bushel	since	November	fifteen	dollars
else	ugly	Wednesday	maple	October
mama	curly	butcher	uncle	white

37

"Look! Here's a pretty pigeon house!
  In every narrow cell
A pigeon with his little wife
  And family may dwell."

pig′eon
nar′row
dwell

38

Every Saturday Henry did the different errands very quickly. Then he had nothing else to do the remainder of the day.

dif′fer ent
er′rands
quick′ly
noth′ing

39

The poplar tree is so tall and straight that it does not give very much shade. At every gust of wind the leaves shake and shiver, as though they would fall to the ground.

pop′lar
straight
shade
shiv′er
though

40

The fir, pine, cedar, and spruce trees wear their green leaves during the entire year. Their twigs are as green in February and March as they are in May.

fir
ce′dar
spruce
wear
twigs

Review

canary	skating	often	finger	dozen
fifty	voices	yard	minute	paper
merry	dear	candle	sleep	yellow

41

The American bison, called by most people the buffalo, is a wild ox. Years ago it was found in our country from ocean to ocean.

A mer′i can
bi′son
buf′fa lo
o′cean

42

Buffaloes feed on grass and chew a cud like the cow. They always seek a valley near the edge of some stream, so that the herd may get both food and drink.

val′ley
edge
stream
herd

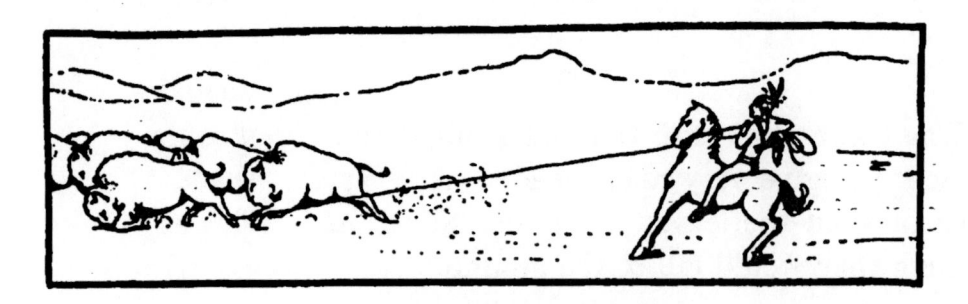

43

When the white men came to this country, they built their homes on the plains near streams. Then they began to kill these animals for their fur and their flesh.

built
plains
be gan'
an'i mals

44

The buffaloes went West, where the Indians caught many of them by throwing a rope over their horns. Now we have no buffaloes except those found in our parks.

In'di ans
throw'ing
o'ver
ex cept'

Review

carry	soap	pencil	flower	farmer
flock	weak	young	months	please
money	father	cheek	while	bird

45

As I passed the grocer's I saw thirteen or fourteen melons in the window. I did not see any berries.

thir'teen
mel'ons
win'dow
ber'ries

46

When I went to market, I saw tomatoes which weighed half a pound apiece. Do you ever go to market? Agnes and I go every morning at eight o'clock.

mar'ket
to ma'toes
weighed
Ag'nes

47

Louise met Margaret on the street and said, "Will you come to my house at four o'clock to help me with my examples? I think my answers are all wrong."

Lou ise'
Mar'ga ret
an'swers
wrong

48

William bent the blade of this knife so much that he broke it. He is very sorry, because his grandma who is dead, gave it to him on his eleventh birthday.

Wil'liam
bent
blade
knife
e lev'enth

Review

children	south	pound	mouth	week
follows	wherever	clock	speak	Friday
morning	flesh	forget	quart	coat

49

"List to the gentle patter
  On each wee blade of grass,
  As it is bent, and back again,
Whene'er the fairies pass."

list
pat'ter
wee
when e'er'

50

Last Wednesday we went to Coney Island by boat. It is only a short sail from New York, but the ship was loaded with people, and we had a very rough trip.

Co'ney
is'land
ship
load'ed
rough

51

On Sunday and every holiday we have either turkey or chicken for dinner. We all like this dinner better than any other.

hol'i day
ei'ther
tur'key
chick'en

52

When Emily is nineteen, her father has promised to let her travel for a year. Isn't it strange that he will let her stay away from home such a long time?

Em'i ly
prom'ised
trav'el
strange

Review

clothes	spell	queer	fried	fresh
fourteen	why	gate	once	right
nearly	February	coal	sting	just

53

There were forty angry geese flying here and there, trying to get away from the dog. He wanted to drive them into that dirty water.

for'ty
an'gry
geese
dirt'y

54

Hear the steam cars whistle as they fly down the track! I am sure that eighty trains pass here each day. Sometimes the noise almost makes me deaf.

steam
whis'tle
track
eight'y
deaf

55

When I went to market on Saturday, I bought a peck of potatoes, some onions, and a few peppers. The grocer said very politely, "Shall I send them for you?"

peck
po ta'toes
on'ions
pep'pers

56

I sat by my window one night,
And watched how the stars grew high;
And the earth and sky were a splendid sight
To a sober and musing eye.
— LONGFELLOW.

splen'did
so'ber
mu'sing

REVIEW

coffee	wolf	hear	other	gallon
great	fruit	comb	storm	Saturday
orange	robin	half	work	fear

57

This is the sixth lace collar I have made since April. I hope to finish it by Tuesday. Your friend, Miss Lamb, said she would give me seventy cents for it, but I think that is not enough.

sixth
col'lar
fin'ish
e nough'

58

I am going to Brooklyn at four o'clock. It is a long distance, and I fear I shall be very tired.

go'ing
Brook'lyn
dis'tance
tired

As correct enunciation is an aid to spelling pronounce the following list of words carefully: *our, was, what, drawing, been, just, pour, poem, singing, umbrella, once, which, saw.*

59

In June we sold ninety yards of red, white, and blue ribbon. It was useful both for Flag Day and for Fourth of July.

nine′ty
rib′bon
use′ful
fourth

60

All the front rooms in our house are much larger than the rear rooms. I know that it takes an hour to sweep each one.

front
lar′ger
hour
sweep

Review

coming	story	school	party	write
ground	workers	keep	street	heat
parlor	hair	handle	laid	seat

61

Alice and Helen were on the lake during the heavy shower. Whose fault was it that they were caught in the storm and nearly drowned?

heav′y
show′er
fault
drowned

Make a list of all words on this page having two syllables. Mark the accented syllables. Take the *ed* from drowned. Remember that the simple word *drown* and the word in Lesson 61 both have but one syllable.

62

There are no fairy folk that ride
About the world at night,
Who give you rings and other things   folk
To pay for doing right.   world
But if you do to others what   blest
You'd have them do to you,
You'll be as blest as if the best
Of story books were true.
— ALICE CARY.

63

To-morrow I expect to go to a small town,   to'-mor'row
sixty miles from here. I hope it will be pleas-   six'ty
ant, so that Frank and I may go down to   pleas'ant
the beach and gather shells.   shells

64

When I brushed my clothing, I found   cloth'ing
that my sleeve was torn about an inch   sleeve
above the elbow. Please wait until I find   el'bow
needle and thread to mend it.   nee'dle
   thread

REVIEW

crazy	string	lake	pear	house
head	afraid	cried	sweet	seven
peach	September	Helen	apples	made

Write 5 words that end in *ead*.

Third Year — Second Half

We may shorten or contract some words by omitting one or more letters. When we do this we use the apostrophe (') to show that something has been left out. Copy the following contractions, with the complete word or words beside each one.

I'm	= I am	isn't	= is not
we've	= we have	they're	= they are
can't	= can not	it's	= it is

Remember that the only time it's is written with an apostrophe is when it means *it is*. When we use it in such sentences as *The bird broke its wing*, we must be careful to write *its* without the apostrophe.

Write the following contractions, and beside each one place the complete word or words:

I'll	we'll	'twas	she's
I've	they've	don't	'twill
she'll	we're	they'll	ne'er

There are titles of honor and respect that we shorten or abbreviate when we use them with the name of a person. Write such abbreviations with capitals, and place a period after each one.

Mr.	= master	Col.	= colonel
Mrs.	= mistress	Gen.	= general
Dr.	= doctor	Capt.	= captain

There are other abbreviations which we often use. These are not written with capitals, but must be followed by a period.

doz.	= dozen	yd.	= yard
pt.	= pint	in.	= inch
qt.	= quart	ft.	= foot
gal.	= gallon	ct.	= cent or cost
bbl.	= barrel	lb.	= pound

The Latin word for *pound* is libra.

Third Year — Second Half

Stamford, Conn.,
Aug. 29, 1915.

Dear Mother,

In a few days it will be time for me to come home, so this is my last letter. I shall be sorry to leave Uncle Will and Aunt Emma. They have been very kind to me. Last Thursday we all went fishing and caught some bass.

How are my rabbits? Has Nora fed them every day? Please take good care of them, and tell all the boys I am coming home soon.

Your affectionate son,
Walter.

Hinsdale, Ill.,
Mar. 20, 1916.

Dear Uncle James,

Mother wishes me to write and say that we shall start for Denver next Tuesday. Papa will go later, as he has some business to attend to.

Thank Alma for the pretty postals she sent me. Now that I have seen pictures of the streets and parks of Denver, I am very anxious to see the places themselves.

Your loving niece,
Margaret Horne.

FOURTH YEAR — FIRST HALF

1

Some time during Sunday night, a thief went into our garden and picked all the ripe vegetables. Monday morning it seemed as though he had also destroyed every leaf and flower.

{ thief
{ thieves
veg′e ta bles
seemed
des troyed′

2

Boughs are daily rifled
   By the gusty thieves,
And the book of Nature
   Getteth short of leaves.
    — Thomas Hood.

boughs
{ day
{ dai′ly
ri′fled
gus′ty
na′ture

3

The peas became yellow and the shell turned yellow. "All the world's turning yellow," said they. Suddenly the shell was torn off by some one's hand, and put into the pocket of a jacket. — Andersen.

peas
be came′
sud′den ly
pock′et
jack′et

4

I like books. I was born and bred among them and have the easy feeling, when I get in their presence, that a stable-boy has among horses.

— Oliver W. Holmes.

bred
eas′y
feel′ing
pres′ence
sta′ble

Review

Alice	ninety	hundred	Easter	amount
drowned	American	onions	hungry	eighty
holiday	easily	among	ostrich	parent

5

Between the dark and the daylight,
When the night is beginning to lower,
Comes a pause in the day's occupations,
That is known as the children's hour.

— Henry W. Longfellow.

day′light
be gin′ning
low′er
pause
oc cu pa′tions

6

The fruit of the milkweed is a tough pod which holds many dozens of little silky threads. At the end of each thread is a tiny brown seed, which flies away when the pod bursts open.

milk′weed
tough
silk′y
{ fly
{ flies
bursts

Draw a line through the silent letters in *known, each, thread, easy*.

7

Did you ever see a bird picking up grains of wheat in the farmer's field? We eat the same food, but the miller grinds it into flour for us, and finally it is baked into bread.

wheat
mil′ler
grinds
flour
fi′nal ly

8

Martha went to the kitchen to see whether she could be of any use. Her mother who stood near the table said, "Please put those lemons, oranges, and melons on the shelf near that large pineapple."

Mar′tha
kitch′en
wheth′er
stood
pine′ap ple

REVIEW

animals	answer	ninth	journey	enough
either	elbow	because	pepper	knife
people	Indians	eleventh	berries	perhaps

9

Let us do our duty in our shop, or our kitchen, the market, the street, the office, the home, just as well as if we stood in the front rank of some great battle.

— THEODORE PARKER.

{du′ty
{du′ties
shop
of′fice
rank
bat′tle

10

When Richard I was king of England, Robin Hood and his merry men lived in the beautiful Sherwood Forest. They dearly loved its hills, its valleys, its flowers, and its carpet of bright green.

Rich'ard
Eng'land
beau'ti ful
for'est
car'pet

11

These men searched and frightened people passing through the woods, and killed four or five of the king's deer every day. Robin Hood never attacked a woman, and always gave a fair amount of the booty to his men.

searched
fright'ened
at tacked'
{ wom'an
wom'en
boo'ty

Write a statement about Robin Hood. Write a question about Robin Hood. What mark is placed at the end of the statement? What mark is placed at the end of the question? Without looking in the dictionary, tell what you think the word *booty* means.

12

Robin Hood was captain of the band. Little John was second in command. Friar Tuck was another one of Robin Hood's men. Maid Marian also lived in the forest, and cheered them all with her sweet music.

cap′tain
sec′ond
com mand
an oth′er
cheered

Review

birthday	bridge	pigeon	loaf	expect
errands	examples	built	pitcher	Louise
larger	laughed	except	butterfly	pleasant

13

As the ruler desired to see Robin Hood whose men did so much mischief, he went to their forest home. The bold highwayman stopped the king's horse and blew three blasts on his horn. In a trice all his men appeared.

ru′ler
de sired′
mis′chief
blasts
ap peared′

14

The king was so pleased with Robin's wit and wisdom that he cried, "It is King Richard who stands before you." Then he invited the entire band to go home with him, and as they departed Robin Hood rode beside the king.

wis′dom
{ cry
{ cried
stands
in vi′ted
de part′ed
be side′

Fourth Year — First Half

15

Hush, my dear, lie still and slumber,
Holy angels guard thy bed;
Heavenly blessings without number
Gently falling on thy head.
— Isaac Watts.

hush
slum′ber
an′gels
guard
heav′en ly

16

Alfred's manners are quite different from those of David. When Alfred meets me on the street, he raises his hat and bows very politely. David passes as though he were ashamed to see me.

Al′fred
man′ners
Da′vid
bows
a shamed′

Review

cabbage	carrots	potatoes	lilies	field
fairy	family	caught	praise	loaves
lovely	loving	fault	chicken	profit

17

The little girl's mother, who saw her resting on her elbow and looking down the road, knew she could not finish her work that way, so she called to her, "Helen, do not sit there idly dreaming of elves and fairies."

road
knew
i′dly
dream′ing
{ elf
  elves

Draw a line through the silent letters in *knew, guard, road, fault*.

18

Hear the rain whisper,
"Dear Violet, come!
How can you stay in your underground home?
Up in the pine boughs
For you the winds sigh,
Homesick to see you
Are we — May and I."

— Lucy Larcom.

whis′per
vi′o let
un′der-
 ground
home′sick

19

Captain Church has a cargo of hickory and walnut, which he is obliged to deliver in England by the twenty-ninth of January. If all goes well, he may reach the other side before the beginning of the year.

{ car′go
{ car′goes
hick′o ry
wal′nut
ob liged′
de liv′er

How should every line of poetry begin? Mention all the punctuation marks used in Lesson 18. Write a sentence that ends with an exclamation mark. Write a sentence containing a direct quotation.

20

Amy, if you saw a greedy spider on the branch of a tree, wouldn't you believe that you were looking at an insect? And yet the spider is not a true insect, because it has eight legs, and its body is divided into two parts.

A′my
greed′y
spi′der
{branch
{branch′es
be lieve′

Review

church	promised	meal	meddle	front
forty	clothing	collar	quickly	melons
lying	fourth	friends	country	ready

21

Doesn't that spider look queer, running to a place of safety with a big white bundle! This contains her eggs; and her young, when hatched, are content to ride on her back.

run′ning
safe′ty
bun′dle
con tains′
con tent′

22

If you spend a few minutes looking closely at a spider, you will certainly see that there are six points on its back. From these points comes the sticky fluid which makes the spider's dainty web.

close′ly
cer′tain ly
stick′y
flu′id
dain′ty

23

When her work is completed, she hides near by with her foot on a single thread, which is connected with her web. When her prey touches the web, Mrs. Spider runs back quickly and captures it.

com ple′ted
sin′gle
con nect′ed
prey
cap′tures

24

For all the flies were much too wise,
To venture near the spider;
They flapped their little wings and flew
In circles rather wider.
— *Selected.*

wise
ven′ture
flapped
cir′cles
rath′er

Review

cousin	remainder	ribbon	music	happen
fairies	deaf	different	rough	needle
mistake	multiply	gentle	dirty	sample

25

Robert Bruce, king of Scotland, was defeated in six battles. At last his men disappeared, and escaping alone, he hid himself in a barn. He thought he would give up the fight.

Rob′ert
Scot′land
de feat′ed
es ca′ping
a lone′

Write all the words on this page that denote the names of things.

26

As he lay in the barn, he noticed a spider trying to fasten its threads from one beam to another. Six times the spider failed. The seventh time it succeeded.

no′ticed
fast′en
beam
sev′enth
suc ceed′ed

27

When Bruce saw this, he sprang to his feet and exclaimed, "I will not give up. I will not be beaten by a spider." He gathered his soldiers together, met the enemy, and won a great victory.

ex claimed′
sol′diers
{ en′e my
en′e mies
won
{ vic′to ry
vic′to ries

28

The thistle's purple bonnet,
And bonny heather bell,
Oh, they're the flowers of Scotland
All others that excel.
— JAMES HOGG.

this′tle
pur′ple
bon′net
bon′ny
heath′er
ex cel′

Review

distance	Sarah	nineteen	heart	heavy
healthy	divide	says	number	ocean
neighbor	heard	division	divisor	shelf

29

Last Tuesday as we neared the shore, the gulls surrounded our ship. I threw half of my orange into the sea, and several birds tried to seize it at once.

shore
gulls
sur round′ed
threw
seize

30

When Mr. and Mrs. Miller went to the country in July, Thomas was obliged to remain with friends until their return. He meant to be good, but I'm afraid he was often very naughty, crying, "Isn't mother ever coming home?"

{ coun′try
{ coun′tries
Thom′as
re main′
re turn′
meant
naugh′ty

31

Did you ever notice the glory of the heavens? Be sure to look out of your chamber window this evening. See whether you can find the Dipper and the North Star.

{ glo′ry
{ glo′ries
heav′ens
cham′ber
dip′per

Write the following words in a column and beside each one the word we use when we speak of more than one: *heart, shore, country, copy, body.*

Fourth Year — First Half

32

Consider the lilies of the field, how they grow; they toil not, neither do they spin. Yet even Solomon in all his glory was not arrayed like one of these.

— *The Bible.*

con sid′er
toil
nei′ther
Sol′o mon
ar rayed′

Review

shower	George	canary	twelfth	until
travel	sixth	great	candle	cheek
butcher	turkey	sleeve	grocery	ground

33

One day in April as Joseph hurried toward the garden, he called to his sister, "Please help me dig some angle worms. Father is going to take Dick and me fishing. We are sure to catch nine or ten perch."

Jo′seph
hur′ry
hur′ried
to′ward
an′gle
perch

34

Last June I was the guest of Dr. Frank's nephew, whose cottage stands near the margin of a large lake. We had great fun playing in the water. Each little wave seemed to murmur, "Catch me if you can."

guest
neph′ew
cot′tage
mar′gin
mur′mur

35

For 'tis a truth well known to most,   truth
That whatsoever thing is lost,   known
We seek it, ere it come to light,   ere
In every cranny, but the right.   { cran'ny
              — WILLIAM COWPER.   cran'nies

36

Up the airy mountain,
Down the rushy glen,   moun'tain
We daren't go a-hunting   rush'y
For fear of little men;   glen
Wee folk, good folk,   hunt'ing
Trooping all together;   troop'ing
Green jacket, red cap,   feath'er
And white owl's feather.
              — WILLIAM ALLINGHAM.

REVIEW

useful	sixty	head	clock	wear
chew	valley	softens	Helen	clothes
guess	children	visit	soil	inches

37

Once upon a time, a fierce and ugly dwarf found a little baby asleep in the forest. Beside the child was a broken sword. A voice said, "Only a man who is truthful and knows no fear, can mend this sword."

fierce
dwarf
a sleep'
{ ba'by
{ ba'bies
sword
truth'ful

38

The baby, who was called Siegfried, had clear blue eyes and golden hair. All the days of his childhood were spent in the woods, and both his shirt and his shoes were made from the skins of animals.

clear
gold'en
child'hood
shirt
skins

39

He always carried a silver horn, with which he called the birds from their forest home. The savage bears and wolves also made haste to come at his call. Siegfried never knew what fear meant, and when he became a man he was able to weld the sword.

{ car'ry
{ car'ried
sav'age
bears
haste
a'ble
weld

Write the following words in a column, and then write the plural beside each one: *baby, fly, thief, half, elf, wolf.*

40

Before Siegfried started out to see the world, the dwarf said, "Siegfried, you are a fine youth, but there is one thing you do not know." Siegfried was silent a moment, and then said, "What is that?" "It is fear," replied the dwarf.

start′ed
youth
si′lent
mo′ment
{ re ply′
{ re plied′

Review

sour	insect	coffee	wife	William
weigh	splendid	jelly	collect	comb
coal	whistle	steam	kept	learn

41

Near Siegfried's home there was a cave which held some hidden treasures. As he wished to know what fear was, the dwarf told him that he ought to try to slay the terrible dragon that guarded the entrance.

treas′ures
ought
slay
ter′ri ble
drag′on
en′trance

42

The dwarf said to Siegfried, "The dragon's body is like a whale, while his skin is covered with many green scales. He does not stand upright, neither does he walk, but turns and twists his body as he crawls in the dust."

{ bod'y
{ bod'ies
whale
scales
up'right
twists
crawls

43

As Siegfried slew the monster, a drop of the dragon's blood fell upon his hand. It burned like fire, till he put his tongue to it. Then he was surprised to find that he could understand what the birds were saying.

mon'ster
blood
tongue
sur prised'
un der stand'

44

And out again I curve and flow
To join the brimming river;
For men may come, and men may go,
But I go on forever.
— TENNYSON.

curve
join
brim'ming
for ev'er

REVIEW

straight	lemon	cried	wrong	yesterday
window	stream	lie	daisy	dead
coming	written	strong	studied	minutes

45

One Thursday in September, the farmer put a load of celery and lettuce in his wagon, and went to the village. When he sold both these vegetables, he bought some fresh meat and a few yards of cloth.

cel′er y
let′tuce
wag′on
vil′lage
cloth

46

As Miss Roberts left the classroom to meet Mrs. King, who called to see about her son Albert, she said, "I do not wish to leave a monitor. I am quite sure you will all behave well while I am absent."

class′room
Al′bert
mon′i tor
be have′
ab′sent

47

Oysters are protected from high waves by living at the bottom of small bays. From the first of May to the last of August, they produce their eggs. During that time, clams take the place of oysters in our daily food.

oys′ters
pro tect′ed
bot′tom
pro duce′
clams

48

This life is too short and precious to waste it in bearing that heaviest of all burdens, — a grudge. Forgive and forget if you can; but forgive anyway.

— Henry van Dyke.

pre′cious
waste
{ heav′y
{ heav′i est
bur′dens
grudge
for give′

Review

subtract	months	doctor	early	always
wrote	sweep	teacher	o'clock	eighteen
disappear	again	almost	tenth	once

49

When I was down beside the sea,
A wooden spade they gave to me
To dig the sandy shore.
My holes were empty like a cup.
In every hole the sea came up
Till it could come no more.

— R. L. Stevenson.

wood′en
spade
sand′y
emp′ty

50

Last Wednesday when Jane came home from the South and called, "Prince, come here!" the dog tried to give her both paws at once, and showed by his joyful actions that he was glad to see her.

Jane
prince
{ try
{ tried
paws
joy′ful
ac′tions

51

The wheels of a farmer's wagon caught in the mud, and in his trouble he called upon Hercules, who said, "Pray put your shoulder to the wheel, and then I may aid you. Heaven helps those who help themselves." — *Æsop's Fables.*

wheels
troub'le
pray
shoul'der
aid
them selves'

52

In October and November, before our furnace is lighted, we have a grate fire in our sitting-room. Here we gather every evening for a pleasant hour, and each one describes the pictures he sees in the fire.

fur'nace
grate
sit'ting-room
de scribes'
pic'tures

Review

thirteen	orange	mouth	flower	better
autumn	thought	thread	parlor	foes
eleven	fifty	beach	throw	peach

53

Trust no future howe'er pleasant;
Let the dead past bury its dead;
Act, — act in the living present,
Heart within and God o'erhead.
— Henry W. Longfellow.

fu'ture
how e'er'
bur'y
pres'ent
o'er head'

54

There once lived in Rome a lady named Cornelia. She was a woman of great intelligence, and spent all her time in educating her two sons, who grew up wise and strong.

Rome
{ la′dy
  la′dies
Cor ne′li a
in tel′li gence
ed′u ca ting

55

One day a lady who cared only for fine clothes, called upon Cornelia. This lady asked to see her jewels. Cornelia, instead of showing rubies or diamonds, sent for her two sons, and when they approached, said, "These are my jewels."

jew′els
in stead′
{ ru′by
  ru′bies
di′a monds
ap proached′

Mention the names of any jewels you know besides rubies and diamonds. Be sure to spell the words correctly. Rewrite the following sentences so they will tell about more than one: *The lady lived in Rome. I saw a woman and a child. Ruth had a beautiful ruby.*

56

Last Friday Uncle Henry left Chicago at 2:30 P.M. and reached New York at 9:30 A.M. on Saturday. As he had most important business to attend to, he was very glad to pay an extra price to travel on this fast train.

im por'tant
busi'ness
at tend'
ex'tra
price

Review

tired	pear	perfect	fourteen	bushel
break	through	tomatoes	piece	fried
follow	breakfast	broken	to-morrow	quarter

57

Everybody who lives in the woods from the first of January to the thirty-first of December, tells us that each season has its own beauty. Would you believe that the dull winter colors are as lovely as those of the spring and summer?

eve'ry bod y
sea'son
{ beau'ty
{ beau'ties
dull
col'ors

NOTE TO TEACHER. — Many exercises similar to the following will be found valuable for reviews. Compare with Lesson 60 and note that one step is taken at a time.

Write the following words in a column and beside each one the word we use when we speak of one: *beauties, victories, enemies, fairies.*

58

Bertha's mother taught her to mend her own stockings. It was not easy for her to learn to sew, because her needle always broke, and her thread always knotted.

Ber'tha
taught
stock'ings
sew
{ knot
{ knot'ted

59

In July the Atlantic Ocean is often so calm that it looks like a mirror. If you cross in February or March, however, there is a chance that you may run into a blinding snowstorm.

At lan'tic
calm
mir'ror
chance
blind'ing

60

Our teacher, Miss Wild, refused to call upon the pupils who always guessed the answers. She was most careful during the grammar and arithmetic lessons.

re fused'
pu'pils
care'ful
gram'mar
a rith'me tic

REVIEW

queen	thirty	story	sigh	since
several	quiet	write	voice	teach
speak	shoes	raise	reach	touch

Write the following words in a column and then write the singular beside each one: *thieves, flies, duties, rubies.*

Fourth Year — First Half

Book, one object, is singular. *Books*, more than one object, is plural. The plural is usually formed by adding *s* or *es* to the singular; as, hill, hills; fish, fishes. Write the following words in a column, and beside each one write the plural form.

table	valley	box	piano
word	turkey	torch	negro
dress	roof	inch	potato

When a word ends with *y* preceded by a *consonant*, the plural is formed by changing *y* to *i*, and adding *es*; as, liberty, liberties; family, families. Write the following words in a column and beside each one write the plural form.

berry	toy	ferry	lily
history	penny	joy	army
grocery	chimney	kidney	monkey

Some nouns ending with *f* or *fe* form the plural by changing *f* to *v* and adding *s* or *es*; as, life, lives; leaf, leaves. Write the following words in a column and beside each one write the plural form.

knife	loaf	wolf	sheaf
calf	thief	half	wharf
shelf	wife	self	elf

Some words ending in *f* or *fe* add *s* only to form the plural; as, roof, roofs.

Write the following words in a column and beside each one write the plural form.

| belief | reef | safe | waif |
| chief | grief | fife | hoof |

Fourth Year — First Half

Streator, Ill.,
Dec. 10, 1915.

My dear Brother,

Mother thinks I ought to write and tell you how much we miss you. She says you will be home for Christmas, and then hurrah for a jolly time!

I wish you would bring me a package of postal cards, for you know I have never been to New York, and I should like to see pictures of Brooklyn Bridge and Central Park.

With love from all, I am

Your affectionate brother,
Walter.

247 West 95 Street,
New York, April 4, 1916.

My dear Laura,

Yesterday I met your brother, who told me that you were ill and in St. Luke's Hospital. He said that you had broken your ankle and might be away from home for several weeks.

I feel so sorry for you! It must be dreadful to lie in bed with no one to talk to. Next Saturday afternoon I am coming up to see you and hope by that time you will be much better.

Your loving friend,
Florence.

FOURTH YEAR — SECOND HALF

1

Money never yet made a man happy. There is nothing in its nature to produce happiness. That was a true proverb of the wise man, rely upon it: "Better is little with the fear of the Lord, than great treasure and trouble therewith."

— BENJAMIN FRANKLIN.

hap'pi ness
prov'erb
re ly'
Lord
there with'

2

Remember that what you possess in the world will be found at the day of your death to belong to some one else; but what you are, will be yours forever.

— HENRY VAN DYKE.

re mem'ber
pos sess'
death
be long'

3

You find yourself refreshed by the presence of cheerful people. Why not make an effort to confer that pleasure on others? You will find half the battle is gained, if you never allow yourself to say anything gloomy. — Mrs. L. M. Child.

{ your self'
your selves' }
re freshed'
cheer'ful
ef'fort
con fer'
al low'

4

The little flower listened to the oriole's song, until she understood its language. She knew the bird was saying: "Rejoice! Rejoice!"

lis'tened
o'ri ole
un der stood'
lan'guage
re joice'

Review

able	nephew	furnace	connected	angels
colors	absent	noticed	grammar	consider
frighten	complete	actions	obliged	guard

5

In the elder days of art,
Builders wrought with greatest care
Each minute and unseen part;
For the gods see everywhere.
— Longfellow.

el'der
build'ers
wrought
mi nute'
un seen'

Take *est* from *greatest*. Now add *er*. Use these three words.

6

Switzerland is a small country in Europe. It is famous for its high mountains and its many lovely lakes, which nestle in the valleys. The Swiss are fond of freedom, and for that reason love the story of William Tell.

Eu′rope
fa′mous
nes′tle
free′dom
rea′son

7

Switzerland was once ruled by the cruel Gessler. To show the Swiss that they must obey him, he placed his hat on a pole in the public square, and commanded every one who passed to bow the knee.

cru′el
o bey′
pub′lic
square
knee

8

Forty or fifty men obeyed. At length Tell passed beneath the hat, and his friends were dismayed to see that he did not even bend his head. Tell said, "Does Gessler suppose he can make all the Swiss obedient to his will?"

length
be neath′
dis mayed′
sup pose′
o be′di ent

Review

appeared	office	ought	heaviest	daily
contains	cottage	arithmetic	oyster	hurry
guest	heaven	curve	ashamed	pause

9

The soldiers near the pole at once reported Tell's conduct to Gessler, who directed Tell to be brought before him. "You are a very fine archer," said he, "and you shall have a chance to save your life by your skill."

re port'ed
con'duct
di rect'ed
brought
arch'er

10

Tell was informed that if he could shoot an apple from his son's head, his life would be spared. However, if he failed, or injured his son in any way, he should die instantly.

in formed'
shoot
spared
in'jured
in'stant ly

11

Tell selected two arrows, and after putting one in his belt, aimed at the apple and cut it in half. Gessler asked Tell why he had selected two arrows. "The second arrow was for you, tyrant," replied Tell, "had I missed my first shot."

se lect'ed
ar'rows
{put
{put'ting
aimed
ty'rant

12

My country, 'tis of thee,
Sweet land of liberty,
   Of thee I sing;
Land where my fathers died,
Land of the pilgrim's pride,
From every mountain side,
   Let freedom ring.
       — SAMUEL F. SMITH.

thee
{ lib′er ty
{ lib′er ties
pil′grim
pride

REVIEW

Atlantic	peas	pictures	instead	desire
dainty	attacked	asleep	pocket	invited
hurried	deliver	describe	battle	precious

13

Those who visited Mrs. Archer saw at once what an excellent housekeeper she was. The floors were clean, the furniture was polished, and the flowers, books, and pictures gave an air of comfort to her rooms.

ex′cel lent
house′keep er
fur′ni ture
pol′ished
com′fort

14

In the fall when many of my favorite flowers are dying, I think that the woods are pleasanter than the meadows. If I find good company, I enjoy walking until the snow flies.

fa′vor ite
{ die
{ dy′ing
mead′ows
com′pa ny
en joy′

15

The first snowfall has arrived. The children have watched eagerly for it. Now they are anxious to leave their cozy room, and join seven or eight boys who are making a snow man on the sidewalk.

ar rived'
ea'ger ly
anx'ious
co'zy
side'walk

16

The wind blows a gale, but the boys are so excited that their mother will allow them to go out in the bitter cold. The largest boy is twelve, and he will not find it very difficult to care for his brothers.

gale
ex ci'ted
bit'ter
larg'est
dif'fi cult

Review

angle	presence	joyful	kitchen	duty
destroyed	beautiful	produce	protect	knotting
jewel	diamonds	dream	believe	pupils

17

The snow had begun in the gloaming,   gloam′ing
And busily all the night,   bus′i ly
Had been heaping field and highway   heap′ing
With a silence deep and white.   high′way
— J. R. Lowell.   si′lence

18

Did you ever read anything about Florence Nightingale? Both her parents were English, but as she was born in 1820 in Florence, Italy, she was named for the city of her birth.

Flor′ence
night′in gale
Eng′lish
It′a ly
birth

19

When she was a child, she often pretended that her dolls had been injured, and then she would nurse and bandage them. She was very fond of animals too, and her first living patient was a shepherd's dog.

pre tend′ed
nurse
band′age
pa′tient
shep′herd

20

From nursing animals, she passed to human beings, and her chief pleasure was caring for the sick and suffering. Her family had a great deal of money, but she did not care for the enjoyments of the rich.

hu′man
be′ings
chief
pleas′ure
suf′fer ing
en joy′ments

Review

bough	purple	refused	Martha	England
duties	empty	bundle	remain	meant
known	lettuce	enemies	bury	reply

21

In 1854 there appeared in the papers, long accounts of the suffering of the wounded soldiers in eastern Europe. These men lacked not only medicines, but the commonest things needed by the sick and dying.

ac counts'
wound'ed
east'ern
med'i cines
com'mon est

22

Florence Nightingale collected a large amount of hospital supplies, and with thirty or forty nurses prepared to leave England at once. When she reached the Crimea, both officers and men gave her a hearty welcome.

hos'pi tal
{ sup ply'
  sup plies' }
pre pared'
of'fi cers
wel'come

23.

She soon had ten thousand invalids under her care, and had general charge of all the hospitals on the peninsula. Her labors finally affected her health, and she was obliged to return to England.

thou'sand
in'val ids
gen'er al
pen in'su la
la'bors
af fect'ed

24

Here she lived for many years and wrote on the subjects of light, fresh air, warmth, and quiet, in dealing with the sick. Longfellow has written a poem on her relief work in the East. It is called "Santa Filomena."

sub'jects
warmth
deal'ing
po'em
re lief'

Review

business	replied	mischief	exclaimed	celery
entrance	captain	Robert	moment	extra
mirror	escaping	carpet	running	safety

25

Whene'er a noble deed is wrought,
Whene'er is spoken a noble thought,
Our hearts, in glad surprise,
To higher levels rise.

no'ble
spo'ken
lev'els

Compare the words *fresh*, *sick*, and *noble* and use each one in a sentence.

26

Thus thought I, as by night I read
Of the great army of the dead,
The trenches cold and damp,
The starved and frozen camp.

thus
ar′my
trench′es
starved
fro′zen

27

Lo! in that house of misery
A lady with a lamp I see
Pass through the glimmering gloom,
And flit from room to room.

mis′er y
glim′mer ing
flit

28

And slow, as in a dream of bliss,
The speechless sufferer turns to kiss
Her shadow, as it falls
Upon the darkening walls.
— H. W. Longfellow.

speech′less
suf′fer er
shad′ow
dark′en ing

Review

certainly	savage	naughty	needle	flour
feather	circle	search	season	neither
nature	fierce	finally	clear	second

29

The flight of the Monkey People through tree-land is one of the things nobody can describe. They have their regular roads, all laid out from fifty to seventy feet above ground, and by these they can travel at night, if necessary.
— KIPLING.

flight
mon′key
no′bod y
reg′u lar
{ foot
{ feet
nec′es sa ry

30

About nine o'clock one Saturday morning, Lilian's mother asked her whether she'd like to go shopping. "Oh, mother," exclaimed Lilian, "what a question!" Then she ran upstairs to dress, and in her haste nearly knocked down her tiny brother Robert.

Lil′i an
{ shop
{ shop′ping
ques′tion
up′stairs
knocked

31

Joseph asked me to leave the piazza and go to see his fine vegetables. I certainly thought that he knew his business, when I found that the spinach and asparagus were flourishing, and that there were quarts of strawberries on the vines.

pi az′za
spin′ach
as par′a gus
flour′ish ing
{ straw′ber ry
{ straw′ber ries

Fourth Year — Second Half

32

When Bessie does not recite her lessons promptly to her brother, she always copies each sentence very carefully in her composition book. I am sure if she does this very often, she will soon surprise her teacher with perfect lessons.

Bes'sie
re cite'
prompt'ly
{ cop'y
{ cop'ies
sen'tence
com po si'tion

REVIEW

seize	lilies	collar	truthful	shoulder
treasures	seventh	melons	country	cousin
Christmas	trouble	sew	mistake	multiply

33

Sir Walter Raleigh was a famous Englishman, who lived in the reign of Queen Elizabeth. He gained her good will by a very simple act of courtesy. Have you ever heard the story?

Wal'ter
reign
E liz'a beth
sim'ple
cour'te sy

34

History tells us that this queen was about to cross a muddy road, when Sir Walter noticed that she paused for a moment. He took from his shoulders a beautiful velvet cloak and spread it in her pathway.

{ his'to ry
{ his'to ries
mud'dy
vel'vet
cloak
spread

35

Such delicate attention both pleased and surprised the queen, who ordered the young man to appear at court. There she bestowed some of her greatest estates upon him.

del′i cate
at ten′tion
or′dered
court
be stowed′

36

He thinks of you before himself;
He serves you if he can;
For, in whatever company,
The manners make the man.
At ten or forty 'tis the same,
The manner tells the tale;
And I discern the gentleman
By signs that never fail.

serves
tale
dis cern′
signs

— Margaret Sangster.

Review

vegetables	venture	village	violet	captain
different	division	divisor	easily	pleasant
needle	neighbor	ninety	ocean	tough

37

"Is that a man's cub?" said Mother Wolf. "I have never seen one." A wolf accustomed to moving his cubs, can mouth an egg without breaking it, and though Father Wolf's jaws closed right on the child's back, not a tooth scratched the skin.

ac cus'tomed
{ move
  mov'ing }
jaws
closed
{ tooth
  teeth }
scratched

38

The Law of the Jungle, which never orders anything without a reason, forbids every beast to eat man, except when he is killing to show his children how to kill, and then he must hunt outside the hunting grounds of his pack or tribe.
— KIPLING.

jun'gle
any'thing
for bids'
beast
tribe

39

If we separate a unit into any number of equal parts, each part is a fraction of that unit. The word "fraction" comes from a Latin word which means "to break." We have many other words derived from the same root.

sep'a rate'
u'nit
e'qual
frac'tion
de rived'

Show change made in the following words when we add *ing*: *move, close, serve, make.*

40

Last Wednesday my sister Blanche was six years old. She received a doll's carriage and a scarlet cloak. She laughed merrily when she saw her birthday cake on the table, with its six lighted candles.

Blanche
re ceived'
car'riage
scar'let
{ mer'ry
mer'ri ly

Review

stable	onion	enough	whale	wheat
walnut	sticky	ninth	errands	examples
either	waste	stockings	ostrich	parent

41

The earth is the Lord's and the fulness thereof; the world, and they that dwell therein. For He hath founded it upon the seas, and established it upon the floods.
— *The Bible.*

ful'ness
there of'
found'ed
es tab'lished
floods

42

There was once a violent sea fight off the coast of Boston, and Captain Lawrence commanded the American vessel. He was noted for his bravery, and though wounded and dying, cried with his last breath, "Don't give up the ship!"

vi'o lent
coast
ves'sel
bra'ver y
breath

Fourth Year — Second Half

43

Grace Darling was the daughter of a light-house keeper. It was her father's business to keep the light burning in all sorts of weather. They both knew that failure to do this might cause great loss of life.

dar'ling
daugh'ter
keep'er
weath'er
fail'ure

44

One night about eleven o'clock Grace was awakened by loud screams. She knew that the current had driven some ship on the rocks. "Oh, father!" she cried, "there's a wreck in the harbor and the people are calling for help."

a wa'kened
screams
cur'rent
wreck
har'bor

REVIEW

suddenly	people	fairies	family	women
whether	surprised	perhaps	pitcher	field
expect	whisper	wisdom	sword	pleasant

45

The wind swept across the water, and her father said, "It will not be possible to go until morning." At dawn a ship was discovered in the distance, and though they feared the waves would swallow their small boat, nevertheless they started.

swept
pos'si ble
dis cov'ered
swal'low
nev er the less'

46

Grace took an oar, and helped her father until they reached the wreck. Those who were on board crowded into the frail boat, and the sailors, with their precious freight, rowed back to the lighthouse.

oar
board
crowd'ed
frail
sail'ors
freight

47

For Thanksgiving dinner we had a fine big turkey with chestnut dressing. We had onions, turnips, cranberries, and several other things. I thought the pumpkin pie was the best of all. Do you agree with me?

Thanks giv'ing
chest'nut
tur'nips
{ cran'ber ry
  cran'ber ries
pump'kin
a gree'

48

In the French capital, the people are familiar with every sort of dress. It would certainly be a very queer style, that would cause these people to stare.

French
cap'i tal
fa mil'iar
style
cause
stare

Fourth Year — Second Half

Review

taught	nineteen	gentle	healthy	answer
youth	terrible	potatoes	profit	heart
friend	American	among	thief	quickly

49

Clytie was a fair young girl with yellow hair, who always dressed in green. She delighted to wander in the fields, glancing constantly at the sun. "I love the sun," she said, nodding to him, "for he is so beautiful."

de light'ed
wan'der
{ glance
{ glan'cing
con'stant ly
{ nod
{ nod'ding

50

As the breeze caressed her curls, Apollo was sure he had never seen such a beautiful creature. He thought it a pity she should die, so he turned her into the yellow blossom, which we know as the sunflower.

breeze
ca ressed'
crea'ture
blos'som
sun'flow er

51

Tired little baby clouds
Dreaming of fears,
Turn in their air cradles
Dropping soft tears.
Great snowy mother clouds
Brooding o'er all,
Let their warm mother tears
Tenderly fall.
  — Mrs. L. L. Wilson.

cra'dles
{ drop
{ drop'ping
brood'ing
ten'der ly

52

For my vacation I went into western Maryland, where I stayed until harvest. There were eighty head of cattle on the place, besides several turkeys, chickens, and geese. My playmates and I spent many pleasant days in the woods and fields.

va ca′tion
west′ern
har′vest
cat′tle
play′mates
{ goose
{ geese

Review

thistle	rough	holiday	become	bridge
amount	Thomas	Sarah	hungry	Indians
heavy	twelfth	though	thieves	shelf

53

My geography tells me that New York is the largest city on this continent. Its five boroughs contain over five million people, and it owes its importance to its excellent position on the Atlantic coast.

{ ge og′ra phy
{ ge og′ra phies
con′ti nent
bor′oughs
mil′lion
im por′tance
po si′tion

54

The way to wealth is as plain as the way to market. It depends chiefly on two words, — industry and frugality; that is, waste neither time nor money, but make the best of both.

— Benjamin Franklin.

wealth
de pends′
chief′ly
in′dus try
fru gal′i ty

55

Aurora lives very near Apollo, the sun god. She is the goddess of the dawn, and is earth's earliest visitor. Just before Apollo dyes the east, Aurora stretches forth her hand and raises the curtain of the night.

god'dess
ear'li est
vis'it or
{ dyes
dye'ing
stretch'es
cur'tain

56

I care not, Fortune, what you me deny;
You cannot rob me of free Nature's grace,
You cannot shut the windows of the sky
Through which Aurora shows her brighten-
    ing face.   — JAMES THOMSON.

for'tune
de ny'
rob
bright'en ing

REVIEW

threads	sour	knife	laughed	chicken
built	tough	tongue	steam	Louise
journey	candy	caught	toward	straight

57

Our handsome ocean steamers are wholly different from those of twenty years ago. Instead of narrow berths, many of them have fine brass beds, and each steamer has a library where one may spend many pleasant hours.

hand'some
steam'ers
whol'ly
berths
{ li'bra ry
li'bra ries

58

I am sorry you had a headache and could not attend Andrew's party. The children played games, and then sang several songs, while Louise played the piano. Before we went home, we had currant cake and chocolate ice cream.

head'ache
{ pi a'no
{ pi a'nos
cur'rant
choc'o late
cream

59

From the trolley we saw some boys teasing an odd looking old man. We were very much pleased to see the janitor of our house treat these boys so roughly, that they were glad to escape.

trol'ley
{ tease
{ teas'ing
odd
jan'i tor
treat

60

To be a gentleman does not depend upon the tailor or the toilet. Good clothes are not good habits. A gentleman is just a gentle-man, — no more, no less.

— Bishop Doane.

gen'tle man
tai'lor
toi'let
hab'its

Review

studied	subtract	flesh	valley	turkey
thought	thread	teacher	please	visit
until	useful	tomatoes	our	watch

Fourth Year — Second Half

There are some words that form their plurals irregularly.

ox,	oxen	tooth,	teeth
man,	men	goose,	geese
woman,	women	foot,	feet
child,	children	mouse,	mice

Review the abbreviations of Fourth Year, First Half, and add the following:

pk.	= peck	Sec.	= secretary
bu.	= bushel	P. O.	= post office
ct.	= cost	A.M.	= morning
amt.	= amount	P.M.	= afternoon

The letters A.M. are the initials of *ante meridian*, meaning before noon. At noon, we say the sun is on the meridian. The letters P.M. are the initials of *post meridian*, meaning after noon.

There is one very important rule in spelling, that every child should know.

Most words ending in silent *e* drop the *e* before a syllable beginning with a vowel; as, move, moving; change, changing; love, lovable; insure, insurance.

Make the proper change in the following words, and then add *ing*, *able* or *ible:* have, come, reside, sale, cure, reverse, care, describe, write, endure, lodge, devote, make.

Make a list of words from your reader ending in silent *e*, and add to these words some syllable beginning with a vowel.

15 Snyder Place,
Newark, N.J.,
Oct. 22, 1916.

My dear Mildred,

The thirty-first of this month, mother says I may have a party, and I would like you to come and help us celebrate Hallowe'en. I expect Marion and Leila, and perhaps Leila's brother Bert.

We shall duck for apples, and play all sorts of games. You may have your fortune told, too, so be sure to come. I shall expect to see you by eight o'clock.

Your affectionate friend,
Julia.

72 So. Orange Avenue,
Newark, N.J.,
Oct. 24, 1916.

My dear Julia,

Your very kind invitation was received this morning, and you do not know how sorry I am that I cannot accept it.

We have company from the country, and father has bought tickets for the Hippodrome for Hallowe'en.

I know you will have a good time, and I only wish that I could be with you.

Yours lovingly,
Mildred.